MY FIRST BOOK OF
Tagalog Words

Filipino Rhymes and Verses

Liana Romulo
illustrations by Jaime Laurel

TUTTLE PUBLISHING
Tokyo • Rutland, Vermont • Singapore

Author's Preface

The words in this book are probably already familiar to children in Philippine households all over the world, as they are frequently used in everyday language. In choosing these specific words, my intention was to teach preschoolers (with English as a first language) what the words mean and how they're spelled, through illustration and memory-enhancing rhyme. After having *My First Book of Tagalog Words* read to them a few times, children will come away with a more precise understanding of vocabulary they might have already picked up at home.

Family appellations, such as *anak*[1] and *lola*,[2] are easily grasped, as they are most common and registered by children at the heart level. Colloquial expressions, such as *naku*[3] and *ewan*,[4] which are difficult to translate, are finally demystified when accompanied by pictures. References to dishes, like *pansit*[5] and *champorado*,[6] inject a bit of Philippine life and culture into the wordplay. Names of Philippine figures and sites, such as Quezon[7] and Vigan,[8] impart a sense of history. Other words, like *hati*[9] and *galing*,[10] have multiple forms and meanings. In the interest of keeping things simple in this first book of a series, I have chosen to define these words only one way: as the word is most likely to be used among children.

The Philippine alphabet does not include the letters C, F, X, Z, Q, V, and J; however, a great number of words using these letters have been adopted into everyday language from Spanish and American colonizers. These are words, such as *zipper* and *jeepney*. Filipino is the national language of the Philippines, and a standardized dialect of Tagalog.

anak[1] child or offspring
lola[2] grandmother
naku[3] *Naku* is used to express distress, and is similar to the interjection "Oh no!"
ewan[4] *Ewan* is a slang expression that means "I don't know."
pansit[5] noodles
champorado[6] hot porridge made with rice and chocolate, sometimes eaten with dried fish
Quezon[7] Manuel L. Quezon was born in 1878. He served as president of the Philippines from 1935 until his death in 1944.
Vigan[8] Vigan is a historic town in northern Philippines. It was named a World Heritage site in 1999.
hati[9] In its verb form *hati* means to divide something in half; for example, food. As an adjective it means "halved" or "divided." As a noun it might refer to the part in one's hair.
galing[10] *Galing*, as it is used in this book, refers to the boy's excellent performance. As a noun *galing* means "source" or "origin." In its verb form it means to "recuperate from illness."

A is for *anak*,
    which isn't my name,
    but that's what Mama calls me.
    To say "my son"
    would be sort of the same.

1

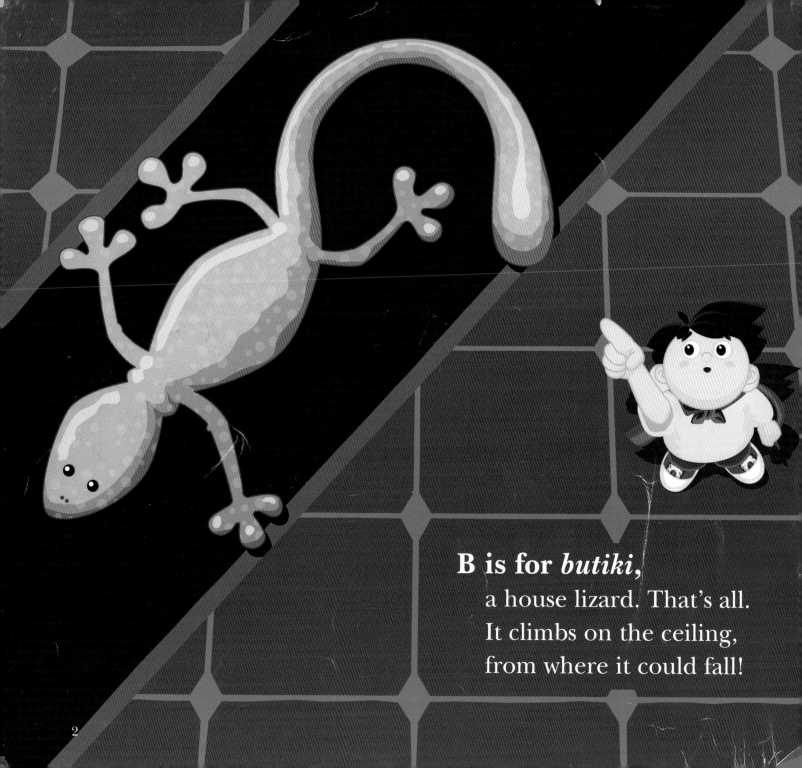

B is for *butiki,*
a house lizard. That's all.
It climbs on the ceiling,
from where it could fall!

C is for *champorado*,
chocolate-and-rice porridge,
believe it or not.
I have it for breakfast.
It's best when it's hot.

3

D is for *dahon*,
leaves rustling coolly in the heat
on trees in our garden, next to
mangoes heavy and sweet.

4

E is for *ewan.*

That's what we say
when we don't know the answer
by the end of the day.

F is for Filipino.
That's what I am.
I was born in the Philippines.
That's me ... in the pram!

G is for *galing*,
always so nice to hear!
A word of praise or approval,
it brings me good cheer.

H is for *hati*,
a word Mama uses at meals,
because it means to share half
with my sister who squeals.

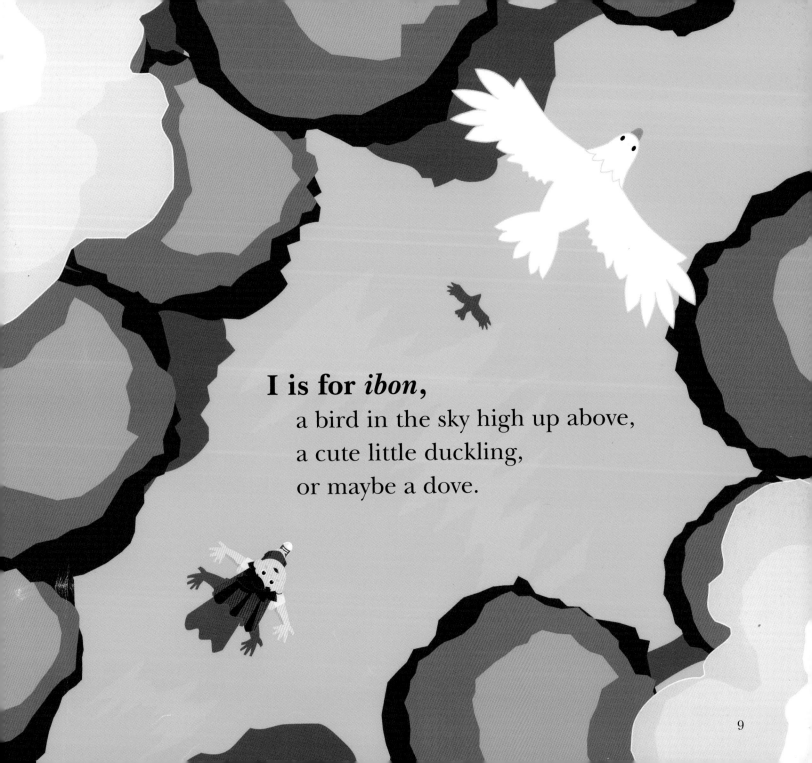

I is for *ibon*,
　a bird in the sky high up above,
　a cute little duckling,
　or maybe a dove.

J is for jeepneys,

miniature buses plying the street.
They're noisy and colorful.
I think they're neat!

K is for *kumot*,
my favorite blanket,
warm in my bed.
And then there's the pillow
to cradle my head.

L is for *Lola*,

who loves me most of all.
She's Papa's mama.
She comforts me when I fall.

12

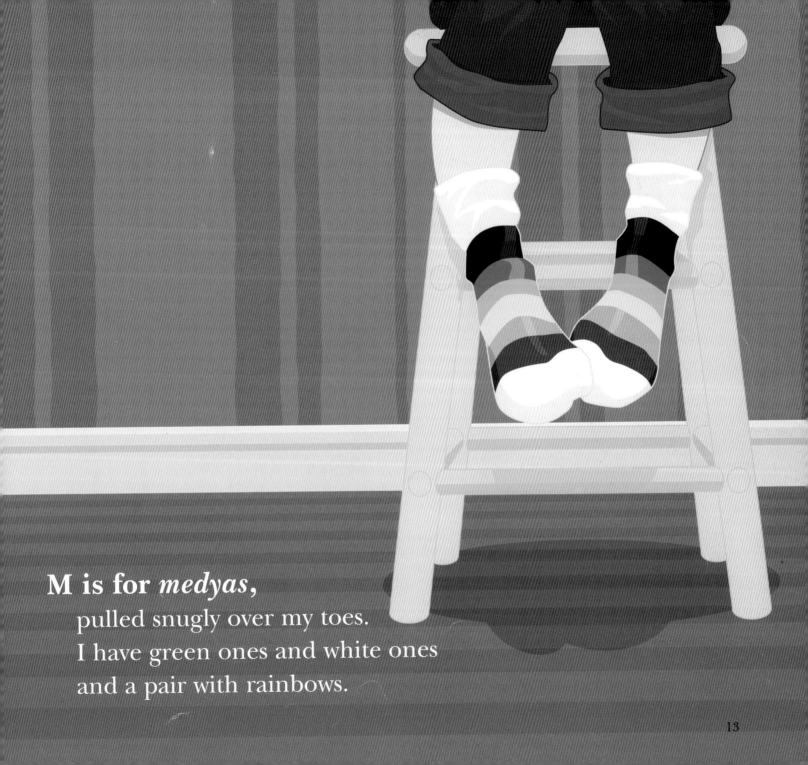

M is for *medyas*,
pulled snugly over my toes.
I have green ones and white ones
and a pair with rainbows.

N is for *naku*!

Just like "oh no!" you'd exclaim
if you broke something precious
or lost in a game.

O is for *ospital*,
   where my sister was born,
   and I brought her a toy:
   a bright yellow unicorn!

P is for *pansit*.
  Oh, noodles, my favorite dish.
  It's nice with pork, beef, or chicken.
  But, please, not with fish!

Q is for Quezon,
president during the Second World War.
Overlooking Quezon City
is a monument to him, therefore.

R is for *relo*,
    a timepiece of any kind,
    so we're always on schedule
    and never run behind.

S is for _salamat_.
That's what we say
when we are grateful.
It's the polite way.

T is for *tahimik*.

"*Shh* ... quiet!" Mama says to me
while praying in church
or reading in the library.

U is for *umaga*,
the end of the night—
when Mama kisses me good morning,
and dark becomes light.

V is for Vigan,
an old northern town
with Spanish-style mansions
and beautiful furniture renowned.

W is for *wala*,
meaning "absent" or "none."
When I wanted a cookie,
Yaya said, "*Wala*, not even one."

X-RAY
ROOM
A

▲ X-RAY ROOM A
◄ X-RAY ROOM B
EXAM ROOM I ▶

X is for X-ray,
just like in English we say.
But in proper Tagalog
it's written *eksrey*.

24

Y is for *Yaya*,
  my nanny, so sweet.
  She loves me like a mother,
  with a tenderness so complete.

Z is for zipper,
a word we hear every day.
But in Tagalog
it's *siper* we say.